GRAPHIC SCIENCE

THE WORLD OF

FOOD CHAINS

WITH

SUPER SCIENTIST

by Liam O'Donnell

illustrated by Cynthia Martin and Bill Anderson

Consultant:
Dr. Ronald Browne
Associate Professor of Elementary Education
Minnesota State University, Mankato

Capstone
press

Mankato, Minnesota

Graphic Library is published by Capstone Press,
151 Good Counsel Drive, P.O. Box 669, Mankato, Minnesota 56002.
www.capstonepub.com

 Books published by Capstone Press are manufactured with paper
containing at least 10 percent post-consumer waste.

Library of Congress Cataloging-in-Publication Data
O'Donnell, Liam, 1970–
    The world of food chains with Max Axiom, super scientist / by Liam O'Donnell;
illustrated by Cynthia Martin and Bill Anderson.
    p. cm.—(Graphic library. Graphic science.)
    Includes bibliographical references and index.
    ISBN-13: 978-0-7368-6839-6 (hardcover)
    ISBN-10: 0-7368-6839-9 (hardcover)
    ISBN-13: 978-0-7368-7891-3 (softcover pbk.)
    ISBN-10: 0-7368-7891-2 (softcover pbk.)
    1. Food chains (Ecology)—Juvenile literature. I. Martin, Cynthia, 1961– ill. II.
Anderson, Bill, 1963– ill. III. Title. IV. Series.
QH541.14.O36 2007
577'.16—dc22   2006035042

Summary: In graphic novel format, follows the adventures of Max Axiom as he explains
the science behind food chains.

Art Director and Designer
Bob Lentz

Cover Artist
Tod Smith

Colorist
Krista Ward

Editor
Donald Lemke

Photo illustration credits: Corbis/Eric and David Hosking, 25; iStockphoto Inc./Sandra
vom Stein, 10; Minden Pictures/D.P. Wilson/FLPA, 17; Shutterstock/Roux
Frederic, 11

Printed in the United States of America in Stevens Point, Wisconsin.
062011   006228WZVMI

TABLE OF CONTENTS

Super Scientist Max Axiom stops at a local outdoor market before an amazing journey into the world of food chains.

Mmmmm.

This apple will satisfy my hunger.

CRRUNCHH!

Just grabbing a quick snack to give me energy for the ride.

You know, all food has energy inside.

Every time we eat a snack or a meal, our bodies absorb proteins, minerals, and vitamins.

FARMERS MARKET

PLEA LI

Every ecosystem on earth contains many food chains.

In most cases, all the energy comes from a single source.

The sun!

But most living things can't absorb this energy directly.

Plants have an amazing ability to turn the sun's energy into food.

This chemical process is called photosynthesis.

DEFINITION

Photosynthesis
(foh-toh-SIN-thuh-siss)
a chemical process by which green plants make their food; plants use energy from the sun to turn water and carbon dioxide into food, and they give off oxygen as a by-product.

Plants are the only producers in a food chain, but there are three types of consumers.

HERBIVORES

Many scientists believe the largest animals to ever walk the earth were herbivores. Measuring 123 feet long and weighing more than 100 tons, the Argentinasaurus ate a lot of plants, including entire evergreen trees!

Consumers that only eat plants, like grasshoppers, are called herbivores.

But other consumers have an appetite for another type of meal.

MUNNCH

MMUNNCH

SQUEEACK!!!

Like this mouse!

SQUEACK!
SQUEEACK!!

Most mice are omnivores. This type of consumer eats both plants and animals.

OMNIVORES

Many animals and insects eat both plants and other animals. Omnivores include most rodents, chickens, raccoons, and even humans. Kodiak bears are the largest omnivores on land. They fill up on grasses and berries, as well as salmon.

The second animal to eat in a food chain is known as the secondary consumer.

The mouse eats the grasshopper and absorbs its energy. The energy from the grasshopper gives the mouse strength to scurry around.

In the deepest, darkest corners of every ecosystem lurks a group of organisms called decomposers.

These creepy, crawly creatures are the final link in every food chain.

DECOMPOSERS

Many remain hidden from other forest dwellers, ready to feed on dead plant and animal parts.

But there's no reason to fear decomposers. They're always in action right under our feet.

Slugs, snails, and fungi are all decomposers.

And they all help break down dead plants and animals into nutrients.

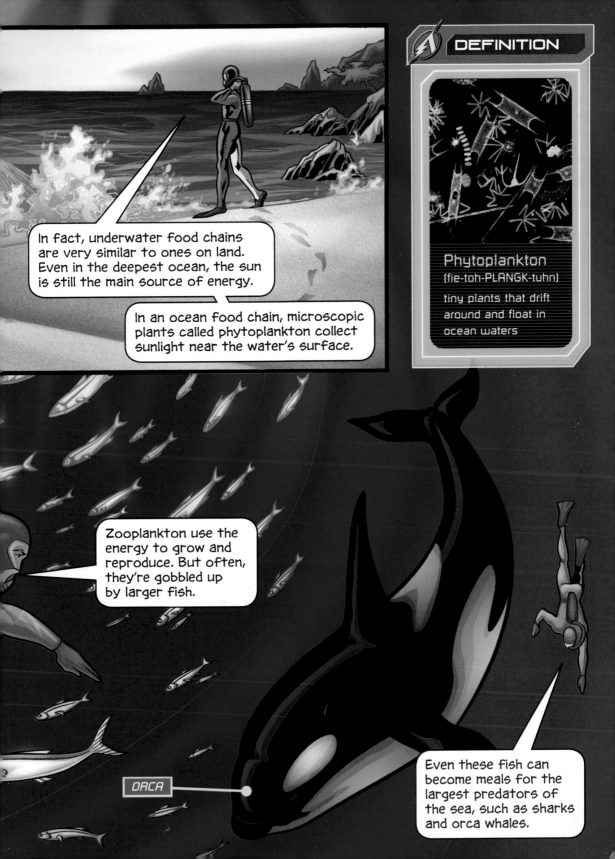

Every ecosystem has many food chains. Often, they overlap and connect into a system called a web.

And no one knows food webs better than my old science teacher, Mrs. Breem.

Hey, Mrs. B! How's the world of science?

Maxwell! My, you've grown. You must have learned to eat your vegetables.

Actually, that's kind of the reason I'm here. I heard your class was studying food webs.

Yes, this is Maria. She's studying the food web of the park.

Hello, Mr. Axiom!

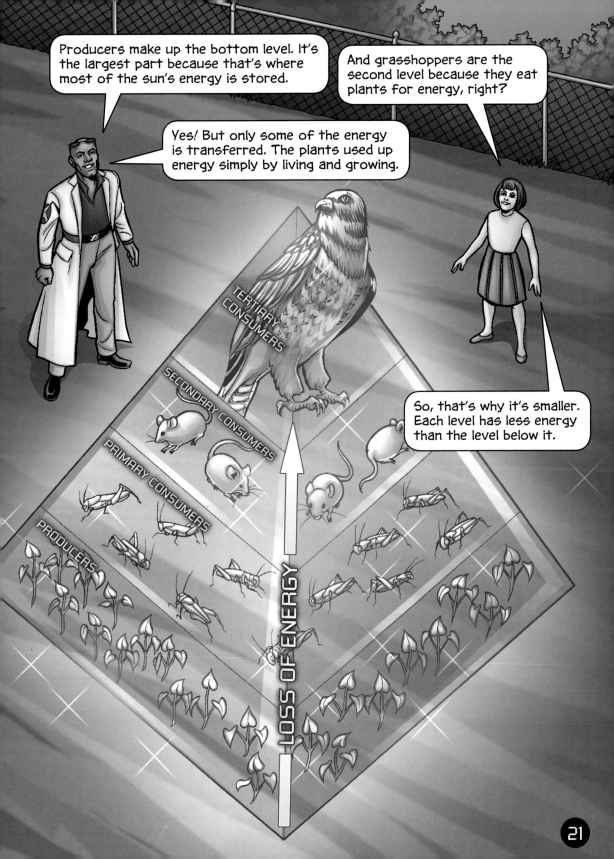

Humans are sometimes responsible for putting a food chain at risk.

Some farms use chemicals to help their crops grow and stay healthy. These chemicals are called pesticides.

Pesticides are too small to see, but they can be very harmful to people and animals.

Pesticides can wash from the farmer's soil into nearby rivers.

Even the fastest birds on earth couldn't escape the impact of pesticides. In the 1940s, the number of peregrine falcons in the United States dropped dramatically. Scientists discovered that peregrines were consuming birds that had eaten insects contaminated with DDT. This pesticide had traveled up the food chain to the top predator. The DDT caused peregrine falcon eggs to thin and break before young could develop. Soon, the falcons were an endangered species. Thankfully, restrictions on DDT have helped the birds make a comeback. Today, they are no longer on the endangered list.

The harmful chemicals are absorbed by producers.

Then, they are transferred from one animal to the next through the food chain.

Pesticides can kill the animals or make them sick.

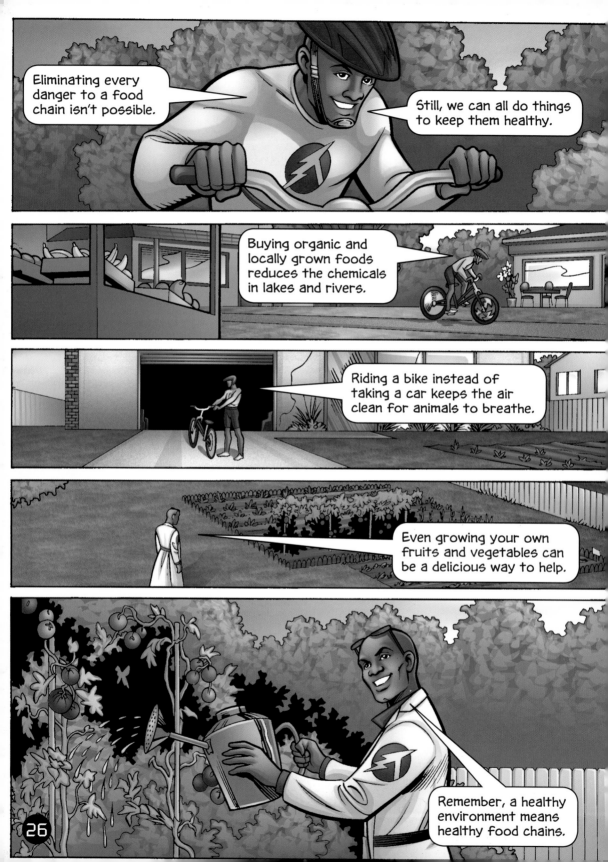

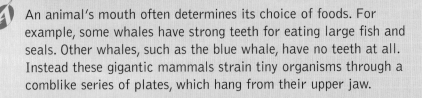

An animal's mouth often determines its choice of foods. For example, some whales have strong teeth for eating large fish and seals. Other whales, such as the blue whale, have no teeth at all. Instead these gigantic mammals strain tiny organisms through a comblike series of plates, which hang from their upper jaw.

Some animals eat only one type of food every day! Koalas in Australia eat nothing but eucalyptus leaves. The koala's picky diet makes their habitat extremely fragile. If eucalyptus trees suddenly disappeared, koalas would have no other food to eat.

Many consumers have amazing abilities and features for capturing their prey. Cheetahs sprint 70 miles (113 kilometers) per hour to snag a rabbit or an antelope. Common loons dive more than 250 feet (76 meters) underwater in search of small fish or leeches. Spiders, such as the garden orb weaver, build strong webs to capture flying insects and even birds.

Scavengers are another important part of food chains and food webs. These animals eat the leftover portions of dead animals. Their bodies break down these larger chunks into smaller bits, which decomposers can then return to the soil.

A parasite is an animal or plant that needs to live on or inside another animal or plant to survive. Parasites aren't usually listed on food chains or food webs. But even top predators can't escape these greedy creatures. Leeches are a parasite that will latch onto animals or humans for a tasty meal of blood.

Carnivores don't have to be large meat-eaters like lions or sharks. Plants can be carnivores as well. Venus flytraps, monkey cups, and other carnivorous plants live where nutrients in the soil are minimal. Instead, these types of plants get food by capturing small prey in their traps.

 Wash what you eat! Farmers often spray vegetables and fruits with pesticides. These chemicals keep pests away in the field but can be harmful to people and animals. Rinsing produce before eating helps eliminate any remaining pesticides and reduces the chance of getting sick.

MORE ABOUT

SUPER SCIENTIST

Real name: Maxwell J. Axiom
Hometown: Seattle, Washington
Height: 6' 1" **Weight:** 192 lbs
Eyes: Brown **Hair:** None

Super capabilities: Super intelligence; able to shrink to the size of an atom; sunglasses give x-ray vision; lab coat allows for travel through time and space.

Origin: Since birth, Max Axiom seemed destined for greatness. His mother, a marine biologist, taught her son about the mysteries of the sea. His father, a nuclear physicist and volunteer park ranger, schooled Max on the wonders of earth and sky.

One day on a wilderness hike, a megacharged lightning bolt struck Max with blinding fury. When he awoke, Max discovered a newfound energy and set out to learn as much about science as possible. He traveled the globe earning degrees in every aspect of the field. Upon his return, he was ready to share his knowledge and new identity with the world. He had become Max Axiom, Super Scientist.

GLOSSARY

carnivore (KAR-nuh-vor)—an animal that eats only meat

ecosystem (EE-koh-siss-tuhm)—a community of animals and plants interacting with their environment

fungi (FUHN-jye)—organisms that have no leaves, flowers, or roots; mushrooms and molds are fungi.

herbivore (HUR-buh-vor)—an animal that eats only plants

nutrient (NOO-tree-uhnt)—a substance needed by a living thing to stay healthy

omnivore (OM-nuh-vor)—an animal that eats both plants and other animals

organic (or-GAN-ik)—using only natural products and no chemicals or pesticides

organism (OR-guh-niz-uhm)—a living plant or animal

pesticide (PESS-tuh-side)—a chemical used to kill insects and other pests that eat crops

predator (PRED-uh-tur)—an animal that hunts other animals for food

prey (PRAY)—an animal hunted by another animal for food

tertiary (TUHR-shee-air-ee)—of third rank, importance, or value

READ MORE

Kalman, Bobbie. *Food Chains and You.* Food Chains Series. New York: Crabtree, 2005.

O'Donnell, Liam. *Understanding Photosynthesis with Max Axiom, Super Scientist.* Graphic Science. Mankato, Minn.: Capstone Press, 2007.

Petersen, Christine. *Conservation.* A True Book. New York: Children's Press, 2004.

Spilsbury, Louise, and Richard Spilsbury. *Food Chains and Webs: From Producers to Decomposers.* Science Answers. Chicago: Heinemann, 2004.

INTERNET SITES

FactHound offers a safe, fun way to find Internet sites related to this book. All of the sites on FactHound have been researched by our staff.

Here's how:
1. Visit *www.facthound.com*
2. Choose your grade level.
3. Type in this book ID **0736868399** for age-appropriate sites. You may also browse subjects by clicking on letters, or by clicking on pictures and words.
4. Click on the **Fetch It** button.

FactHound will fetch the best sites for you!

INDEX